who are the independent catholics?

an introduction to the independent and old catholic churches

by john p. plummer
and john r. mabry

the apocryphile press
BERKELEY, CA
www.apocryphile.org

books by john p. plummer

The Many Paths of the
Independent Sacramental Movement

Living Mysteries: A Practical Handbook
for the Independent Priest

books by john r. mabry

The Way of Thomas:
Nine Insights for Enlightened Living
from the Secret Sayings of Jesus

The Monster God:
Images of Horrific Divinity
in the Religions of the World

Noticing the Divine:
An Introduction to Interfaith Spiritual Guidance

Faith Styles: Ways People Believe

God is a Great Underground River

God Has One Eye: The Mystics of the World's Religions

I Believe in a God Who Is Growing:
Process Perspectives on the Creed,
the Sacraments, and the Christian Life

Crisis and Communion:
The Re-Mythologization of the Eucharist

Heretics, Mystics & Misfits

God As Nature Sees God:
A Christian Reading of the Tao Te Ching

The Tao Te Ching: A New Translation

The Little Book of the Tao Te Ching

who are the independent catholics?

an introduction to the independent and old catholic churches

apocryphile press
BERKELEY, CA

Apocryphile Press
1700 Shattuck Ave #81
Berkeley, CA 94709
www.apocryphile.org

contents

Appendix 3 • Historical Documents

introduction

THIS BOOK ARISES OUT OF A NEED in the Independent Catholic community for a compact and concise introduction to our movement. I can't say how many times I have met with a couple for a wedding, who, after hearing me talk about the movement for quite some time, often ask, with not a small amount of amazement, "Is there a book we can read about this?"

There are, of course, several good books. But most of them are more academically oriented than the lay reader really wants to dig into. Also, almost all of the books available are too expensive for Independent clergy to buy in bulk and hand out as occasion demands.

This is intended to be a book that can introduce interested people to the Independent Catholic movement in a friendly, easy-to-read style that will not tax their patience or their wallets. In fact, we are purposely designing this book to be available at discount prices to Independent Catholic clergy, so that they can buy them in bulk and hand them out to people they meet with for weddings, baptisms, funerals, or other sacramental services.

The Independent Catholic movement is wonderfully diverse, and it is not possible to adequately cover the full spectrum within an introductory volume of this size. Rather, we have focused on the most common varieties of Independent Catholicism in hopes of providing a short, useful orientation to the newcomer. Those who are interested in exploring further will find resources in Appendix 2 (p. 72).

We both have found a home and a place of service within Independent Catholicism. It is a joy and privilege to introduce you to what we have discovered.

—JM & JP

1 • independent catholics
the best-kept secret in catholicism

I (JOHN M.) MET DYLAN AND TERRI at the local Denny's to discuss their upcoming wedding. They were both in their thirties and were nervous and excited about meeting with a priest. Soon we ordered and were able to really get down to business. Dylan had been married before, and Terri was not Catholic. For the sake of Dylan's family, they wanted a Catholic wedding, but were having trouble finding a minister—Catholic *or* Protestant—who would marry them. To top it off, they wanted a full mass, out-of-doors in a redwood grove. They grew more and more nervous as they described what they wanted. I smiled reassuringly throughout their description, and when they finished, Terri said. "So…can you do it?"

"No problem," I told them. Their jaws dropped and they looked at one another in stunned disbelief. They had apparently expected more of what they had heard up to that point: red tape and more hoops than they could possibly jump through to reach their goal. For a few minutes they were speechless

"How is it that you can do this when no one else we talked to could?" Dylan finally asked, by now a little skeptical.

"Well, I don't know who you talked to before, but I'm an Old Catholic priest," I explained, "and our rules are not as strict as some ministers you may have talked to."

"Old Catholic?" Terri said, puzzled. "You don't look old to me!"

"Thank you," I said. I (John M.) am in my mid-forties, and it is awfully nice to be told I'm not as old as I fear I am every time I look in the mirror. "But Old Catholic refers to the *variety* of Catholic, not my age. We're part of a larger movement of Independent Catholics. Have you heard of it?" They both shook their heads, and I leaned in and whispered, "I'm not surprised. We're the best-kept secret in Catholicism."

the romans are not
the only catholics in town

I was not surprised that Dylan and Terri had not heard about Independent Catholicism—our movement is not well-publicized. Nevertheless, there are quite a few of us around. When people hear the word "catholic" they automatically think "Roman Catholic," and this is understandable. Most Catholics people encounter are of the Roman variety and

Roman Catholicism is the largest single body of Christians in the United States. But, in fact, Roman Catholics are not the only kind of Catholics in the world and never have been.

The most visible Catholic churches of the non-Roman variety are the many Eastern Orthodox churches, which are largely national in origin. The Russian Orthodox, the Byzantine Catholic, the Armenian Orthodox, the Greek Orthodox, Syrian Orthodox, and many others—all are Catholics, and all are completely independent of Rome. They call themselves "autocephalous" (self-headed), which simply means, "appointing its own leader."

There are non-Roman Catholics in the West as well. The world-wide Old Catholic Communion broke from the Roman Church in 1724 and has member churches in many European countries (more on them later). Similarly, the Anglican Communion of churches extends to nearly every country on earth. They have the unusual distinction of being both Protestant and completely Catholic.

Independent Catholics are the fastest-growing variety of Catholic in the West. We are found in every city of every state in the U.S. and Mexico, every Province of Canada, and throughout Australia, Europe, and South America. Many pockets of Independents look very much like Romans, some very much like Orthodox, and some very much like Anglicans. And still others are extremely idiosyncratic and look like no one but themselves. Which all begs the question: Exactly what do we mean by "Catholic"?

what makes a church catholic?

There may be as many answers to this question as there are varieties of Catholics, but most of them would agree upon some foundational elements: a profession of faith as articulated in the creeds, the celebration of seven sacraments, the threefold order of ministry, and an unbroken line of apostolic succession. Let's briefly look at what each of these means.

The Historic Faith of the Creeds. The great majority of Catholics uphold the basic tenants of Christian faith as articulated in the creeds. Two creeds that are of most historic importance are the Apostles' Creed and the Nicene Creed (both are found in Appendix 3, pps. 74-75). The Apostles' Creed evolved out of early baptismal formulas, while the Nicene Creed was compiled to reflect the decisions of the Nicene council in 325 CE (reaching its completed form in 381). Nearly all Christians, Catholics and Protestants, value the creeds as basic statements of universal Christian faith—though, admittedly, there is often a broad spectrum of difference in what people *understand* the words of the creeds to mean.

The Celebration of Seven Sacraments. The seven sacraments are physical rituals and elements that we believe mysteriously but certainly convey God's grace to those who participate in them.

The first sacrament is *Baptism*, with is the rite of initiation into the Christian community. For those born into the faith, Baptism usually takes place as a child, but for those who convert later in their lives, Baptism is given whenever a person is ready for it.

Confirmation is the anointing with oil that seals a baptized person as God's own forever. Orthodox Catholics do not separate this ritual from the sacrament of Baptism, but confirm babies as soon as they are baptized. In the West, however, Confirmation is a rite of passage, where children (or adults) who have come of age "own" the baptismal vows made on their behalf when they were children. It is a way for them to publicly profess the faith that they were raised in as children, but are now old enough to embrace for themselves.

Eucharist is the celebration of Christ's continued presence in our midst using the "vehicles" of bread and wine. Catholics believe that Jesus is really and truly present in the celebration of the Eucharist, although different varieties of Catholics will describe this reality in different ways. Eucharist is the central ritual of Christian worship—indeed, few of the other sacraments are performed without it, unless there are extenuating circumstances. Most Catholic Christians take communion at least once a week, and some even do it daily.

Confession is a sacrament in which people can relieve themselves of the burden of sin and guilt they may be carrying. Going to confession is a discipline that reminds us that we are all imperfect human beings who are always in need of forgiveness and grace, both from one another and from God. This is not about seeing ourselves as "bad people," for most of us are not. But few of us, if we are honest with ourselves, ever get through an entire day without thoughtlessly hurting someone's feelings, pursuing our own ends without considering how it will effect someone else, or ignoring someone in need that we could, if we really wanted to, help in some way. This is only human, but still less than what God calls us to be. Confession offers us an opportunity to get honest with ourselves and with God, and to start again with a clean slate.

Marriage is a strange sacrament in that it is one of the few that the laity themselves perform—clergy are really just there as witnesses. Catholic Christians see the mystical union between two people entering into Holy Wedlock as being a symbol—even a sacrament in a broader sense of the term—of Christ's union with the universal church.

Ordination is the sacrament by which members of the church are set apart and given the responsibility to serve their fellow Christians as clergy. It involves both the investiture of the power to perform sacraments and the burden of responsibility as the local community affirms its trust in these individuals to be faithful servants.

Unction is also known as the Anointing of the Sick and the Last Rites. Although anointing a sick person does not mean that person is dying, the ritual actions in both cases are the same, so they fall under the same category of sacrament. In Anointing someone who is sick we represent to God the prayer of the whole church for the ill person, and we apply oil, an ancient symbol of healing, as a tangible expression of that prayer. There is nothing crudely magical about

Anointing the Sick nor about any of the Sacraments. We do not command God to act or to heal anyone. We merely ask, and assure the person receiving the sacrament that God's grace and spiritual healing is assured, even if physical healing is not. The Last Rites is the anointing of a person who is dying, commending that person's soul to God, and assuring the dying person that just as they have been faithful to God in this life, God will be faithful to him or her in the next.

The Threefold Order of Ministry. All Catholics arrange their clergy in a hierarchy, with greater powers and responsibilities for different "orders" of ministry. Deacons have the least amount of power and responsibility. Διακονοσ means "servant" in Greek, and indeed, Deacons typically are called to ministries of service to the poor, the needy, the sick, the imprisoned, or anyone else to whom they can extend their hands as the hands of Jesus. Deacons can preach and perform several of the sacraments: they can baptize, perform marriages, and in Orthodox, Anglican, and many Independent Catholic churches, anoint the sick. Many deacons in the larger churches are not full-time or even paid clergy, but have "day jobs" and perform their duties to the church as volunteers.

Priests are the "middle children" of the Catholic clergy. They are often pastors or scholars, and their duties usually involve teaching, preaching, leading liturgy, parish administration, and visiting sick and dying parishioners. They can perform all of the sacraments that deacons can, plus the Eucharist (also known as Holy Communion or the Lord's Supper) and Confession (although Roman priests must have faculties from a bishop to hear Confessions). In addition, Orthodox priests may Confirm, along with some Roman priests with faculties to do so.

Bishops are the leaders of Catholic churches, and they serve as pastors to both priests and deacons, upholding them and encouraging them in their ministries to God's people. Bishops often also serve as senior administrators for the church structure, though some bishops are "assistant" bishops who assist the main bishop mainly with liturgical duties. Bishops can perform all seven of the sacraments, adding to the lists of deacons and priests the ability to Ordain clergy for the church.

An Unbroken Apostolic Succession. Catholics believe that when Jesus consecrated his apostles, he placed his hands upon their heads and conferred upon them both the power and the authority to continue his mission in the world. As those apostles went on their missionary journeys to different parts of the world, they did the same thing, laying their hands on the heads of those that they were consecrating as local bishops to continue Christ's ministry in that place. Those bishops, before they died, consecrated new bishops to carry on their work, and so on, right down to the present day. Catholics see this unbroken chain of consecration, going all the way back to Jesus himself, as a valuable gift that God has given to the church as a way to safeguard it from error and as a witness to Jesus' continued presence and action in— and on behalf of—the world.

It may seem strange to say that the apostolic succession safeguards the church from error, since it is true that people in the various Catholic churches often strongly disagree with one another about things that look like trivialities to outsiders. And in fact, they are trivial indeed. The fact that such things divide us only testifies to the fragility of human nature and the profound need for the grace of God that we all experience. And how is it that the church is safeguarded from error when even a cursory examination of church history reveals that people taught—and believed—very different ideas about who Jesus was, how salvation is effected, the exact meaning of the sacraments, etc.?[1]

St. Augustine settled the question by laying a very heavy emphasis on the importance of the unbroken apostolic succession. As long as someone is ordained in the succession, he contended, it does not matter whether their teaching is in error, or even if the clergyperson is a particularly moral person—their sacraments are still valid. Catholic churches everywhere have taken solace in Augustine's formulation. Because every church is made up of fallible human beings, every church has had to contend with clergy that were less than moral or less than orthodox in their teaching. According to Augustine's theology, we can rest assured that a few bad apples do not spoil the whole barrel—God is still at work in the church, and the succession of bishops from Jesus himself is a visible and certain witness to this fact.

jurisdictions, not denominations

The ultimate unity of the Catholic faith is attested to by the fact that Catholics are not divided into denominations, as Protestants are, but into jurisdictions.[2] There is only "one holy Catholic and apostolic Church," but for reasons of pragmatic administration—and often prideful and sad human history—this One Church is governed by many criss-crossing regions of administration.

These jurisdictions are sometimes geographical and sometimes ideological—and usually, to some degree or another, both. For instance, here in the city of San Francisco, we see the intersection of various Catholic jurisdictions: the Roman Catholic Archdiocese of San Francisco, the Episcopal Diocese of California, the various jurisdictions of the many ethnic Orthodox churches, the separate jurisdictions of various Roman, Orthodox, Anglican, and Old Catholic religious orders (all of which are distinct from diocesan jurisdictions), and, of course, the many overlapping Independent Catholic jurisdictions. We are all Catholics, and all part of the "one holy Catholic and apostolic Church," yet for reasons of history and practicality, we fall into different structures of hierarchy and administration. The word "catholic" comes from the Greek word καθολικοσ, which means "according to the whole," or "universal." The various Catholic communions taken as a whole come much closer to describing this "universal" church than any of them can do individually.

why independent catholicism?

Independent Catholics may be the smallest, and therefore, least visible of the various Catholic jurisdictions, but we are growing fast and are meeting important needs that sometimes fall through the cracks of our bigger sister churches. Because rules and regulations differ for every jurisdiction, Independent Catholics can sometimes bring the sacraments to people in ways the larger churches cannot.

For instance, as an Old Catholic priest, my jurisdiction does not prohibit remarriage, marriage between Catholics and non-Catholics, nor weddings out-of-doors. For these three reasons alone, I was happy to be able to serve Dylan and Terri and many others in my nearly fifteen years of priestly ministry. This is a joy that many Independent Catholic clergy share. The ability to serve those who have felt rejected or alienated from the larger churches is one reason why so many people are seeking vocations as Independent Catholic clergy.

Many Independent clergy have already had long careers as priests or religious in our big sister churches, but have had to leave active ministry in those communions to marry or to follow their consciences in other ways not possible in their communities of origin. Most Independent jurisdictions allow married clergy, many ordain women, and some allow full inclusion of gay and lesbian people in all levels of ordained ministry. Since gender or sexual orientation (or even the ability to exercise one's sexuality at all) are often a barrier in some of the larger Catholic bodies, the Independent movement offers a place where a person's true vocation to ministry can flourish.

Sexuality is not the only reason people are attracted to the Independent movement, of course. Some people cannot afford the steep cost of mainstream seminary, others have been prevented from proceeding to ordination in other communions due to unfortunate circumstances. Still others are attracted because the Independent movement is extremely tolerant of diverse and idiosyncratic approaches to ministry and spirituality.

The Church is more than clergy, of course. Because of the loving and welcoming attitude of Independent communities, many laypeople are discovering that the Independent Catholic movement is a valuable place for them to practice their faith and exercise their service to God as Catholic Christians. Because of the vast diversity that exists within the Independent movement, those people who are unhappy with—or estranged from—the larger churches can more than likely find exactly what they are looking for. Traditionalists can find Masses in Latin, while those seeking justice for women and sexual minorities will find communities that welcome people of all genders and sexual orientations. Those who practice Zen Buddhism will find services where they can meditate and then take communion, and every other possible combination.

membership in
independent catholic communities

Some people worry that receiving a sacrament from us will somehow "change them" from their current identity and "make them" an Independent Catholic. This is not true, however. Receiving a sacrament from an Independent Catholic clergyperson does not make one an Independent Catholic. It just affirms our essential unity as members of the "one holy Catholic and apostolic Church," which, as we have seen, has many jurisdictions.

If one wants to become an Independent Catholic, it is as easy as joining any other church. Just start coming! Talk with your deacon, priest, or bishop about membership, and, if you have not been baptized or confirmed before, about participating in those sacraments with the loving support of your community. Feel free to volunteer your time or talents, as most Independent Catholic churches are small communities and there are lots of things that need to be done. But be careful not to take on too much too soon, and be sure you are comfortable saying "no" when your plate is full. Everyone will understand, as their plates are usually pretty full as well.

are independent catholic
sacraments appropriate for everyone?

No, just as not all of the larger jurisdictions' ministries are right for everyone. As clergy we are here to serve God's people, but only you can say if what we have to offer is appropriate for your unique situation.

Like Dylan and Terri, it may be that you have hit some roadblocks with the larger churches. Perhaps you want a priest whose spirituality is more like your own. Or perhaps it is more important to members of your family than it is for you that you arrange a traditional wedding, baptism, or funeral service. If you are not involved with a local Roman Catholic, Orthodox, or Anglican parish, this can often be a problem. Or perhaps you want to craft a creative ceremony that falls outside the bounds of what other priests or ministers feel comfortable doing. In these cases and lots of others, an Independent Catholic clergyperson may be just right.

Keep in mind, however, that due to the brokenness inherent in all human institutions—especially religious ones—people do not always esteem others as they ought to, and some churches do not recognize the authority or validity of other churches. For instance, the Roman Catholic Church, while only grudgingly acknowledging the validity of Orthodox sacraments, completely denies the validity of our Anglican brethren. Roman, Orthodox, and Anglican perspectives on Old Catholic ministry run the gamut from full acceptance to outright rejection, and there is often not a consistent policy within these groups regarding Independents. Sometimes clergy in the bigger churches simply dismiss Independents out of hand because they have not heard of us or are ignorant of our history.

Regardless, it is doubtful that the larger churches are going to be pleased if you go outside of their "system."

In fact, by doing so, you may be technically breaking some of the rules of your institution. If you are not a member of any of the larger churches, this will probably not concern you in the least. But if you are, it is important that you be fully aware of the facts before you proceed. No one will be excommunicated for receiving the Eucharist from or being married by an Independent Catholic priest, but nor will the Roman Catholic Church esteem an Independent Catholic wedding in exactly the same way as one performed by one of their own priests. The Anglicans and many Orthodox are often more generous on these issues.

why is it that so few people know about independent catholics?

This is a question I hear a lot, and it's simply because we are small. Our worshipping communities, likewise, are small, and as a movement, we own few buildings. Most Independent Catholic churches are house churches, where the Eucharist is often celebrated by a local bishop consecrated for ministry to that community. In this, our churches are very similar to the earliest Christian communities, which often met in houses and were gathered around the local bishop. But as we are growing, the word is getting around.

If you open the phone book in almost any major city in the United States, you will find several varieties of Catholics there aside from those of the Roman variety. They will go by a diversity of titles, such as "Catholic, Old," "Catholic, Celtic," "Catholic,

Ecumenical," or "Catholic, American," or almost any other conceivable name paired with "Catholic." The same is true for many churches with "Orthodox," "Anglican," "Episcopal," or "Sacramental" in their titles. Many of these are churches of the Independent Catholic movement, and visiting them will treat you to a wide variety of services and ministries.

By this time, you may be asking how such an unusual and diverse movement ever got started—especially when it is part of Catholicism, which people normally think of as being very strict, even monolithic. In our next chapter we will look at the history of the various Independent Catholic communities, where they came from, and where they are today.

2 • history
where did we come from?

AS WE HAVE SEEN IN THE FIRST CHAPTER, Independent Catholicism has been a very well-kept secret. When most of us hear the words "Catholic," "Anglican," or "Orthodox," we immediately think of the large mainstream jurisdictions which use these names. After a new visitor has asked, "Who are you?" the next question is usually, "Where did you come from?" This is a very natural question for visitors from larger Catholic jurisdictions, who are surprised to find small independent communities claiming a Catholic identity, and a ministry in apostolic succession.

The roots of the Independent Catholic movement are diverse, and many different groups have mingled over the centuries. Most communities in the United States today can trace their ancestry to a number of different sources. A complete consideration of all the sources of the movement is beyond the scope of this book, but we will look at several of the most important parts of our history, beginning with the earliest origins in Dutch Old Catholicism.

varlet and mathew

In the late 1600s, Holland was a primarily Protestant country, although with tolerance for a Catholic minority population. As the government was Protestant and had no interest in enforcing policies of the Roman Church, it became a safe place for Roman Catholic clergy who were having theological or other difficulties. A number of priests who were associated with a movement called Jansenism moved to Holland. Jansenism was a teaching on grace and free will which the Roman Church thought was too similar to Luther and Calvin.

The Archbishop of Utrecht, Pieter Codde, may not have been a Jansenist himself, but he supported his clergy, and would not sign the official condemnations of Jansenism. As a result, Rome removed Archbishop Codde in 1702, although the Dutch church did not accept this decision and Codde continued to lead the church until his death in 1710. After his death, Roman authorities refused to provide a new bishop for the city of Utrecht. While Jansenism was the point where the dispute started, the problems between Rome and Utrecht were really about the freedom of the local community from central authority.

In 1719, a French missionary bishop named Dominique-Marie Varlet was on his way to his new assignment in the Middle East, when bad weather forced him to land in Holland. He took pity on the Dutch Catholics and performed some confirmations for them before journeying on. After he got to the Middle East, Rome summoned him back to Europe to answer for these Dutch confirmations and his failure to sign the condemnation of Jansenism. Varlet returned to Holland where he stayed the rest of his life.

In 1724, Varlet consecrated a new bishop, Cornelius Steenhoven, for the Dutch church. He had been properly elected by the local clergy as their bishop, but Rome would not approve him. Varlet also consecrated three other bishops for the Dutch church before his death in 1742. Rome excommunicated everyone involved in these consecrations. The 1724 consecration of Steenhoven marks the beginning of the independent Dutch Catholic Church, under the Archbishop of Utrecht, which continues to the present day.

After the 1724 break with Rome, the Dutch church carried on quietly for some time. Then, in 1869, the (First) Vatican Council of the Roman Catholic Church opened. There was a push to define the infallibility of the pope as an official teaching of the church. Opponents of this teaching started calling themselves "Old Catholics," as they believed this to be a new teaching, and not the way of the ancient church. In 1870, the Council voted to define papal infallibility as a required teaching of the Roman Church. Many Catholics in Germany and Switzerland were deeply troubled by this move. The Dutch church stepped forward and helped these communities form "Old Catholic" communities separate from Rome. Dutch bishops ordained priests and consecrated bishops for these communities, making sure that Catholic apostolic succession was preserved. Today, there are still very many Old Catholic communities in Central Europe, where they are often larger and better known than in the United States.

In 1896, the pope issued a decision which said that the apostolic succession of the Church of England (the Anglicans) was not valid. This obviously upset many Anglicans, who valued their place within the larger Catholic tradition. Rome did accept the apostolic succession of the Old Catholics on the continent, so some Catholic-minded Anglicans started thinking that a connection to Old Catholicism might solve the problem.

Arnold Harris Mathew was an Englishman born in France in 1852. He had served as a priest in the Roman Church, and later (after marriage) in the Anglican Church. He was also a good friend of a number of members of the Catholic "modernist" movement that sought to bring Catholic theology into dialogue with contemporary thought. After correspondence with the Dutch bishops, they decided to consecrate Mathew as a bishop for a British mission in 1908. During this time, the Dutch bishops were very mission-minded, and also helped to start the

Polish National Catholic Church in the United States, and the Mariavite Church in Poland.

Mathew's mission in Britain got off to a slow start, and he eventually broke with the Dutch bishops over some ordinations and consecrations which they had not approved. Again we see the same tensions between centralized authority and local independence which had led to the formation of the Dutch church now replayed in England. Mathew consecrated many bishops, and his church became the direct ancestor of literally dozens of independent communities in the UK and US.

ferrette and vilatte

The vast majority of Independent Catholics in the United States can trace their history not only to the Dutch Church through Bishop Mathew, but also to the Syrian Orthodox Church, through two missionaries to the West, Jules Ferrette and Rene Vilatte.

Jules Ferrette was a former Roman Catholic priest who had become a Protestant missionary in the near East. While valuing his independence from Rome, he thought it would be desirable to restore apostolic succession and a connection to the Catholic tradition to his Protestant colleagues. An opportunity arose when, through a translation project, he became friends with Moutran Boutros, the Syrian Orthodox bishop of Emessa. He shared his dreams with Moutran Boutros, who consecrated Ferrette as a missionary bishop for England in 1866. Ferrette journeyed to England and worked without a lot of visible success until his death in 1904. He would have been heartened to see that many of his spiritual descendents have been much more successful in bringing an autocephalous Catholicism to life.

Rene Vilatte was also French and a former Roman Catholic who became a Protestant missionary, in his case, to Wisconsin. Vilatte corresponded with a European Old Catholic priest and theologian named Hyacinthe Loyson, who was also a friend of Arnold Mathew. With help from Loyson, and the support of the local bishop of the Episcopal Church, Vilatte journeyed to Europe, was ordained as an Old Catholic priest, and charged to be a missionary to the Belgian and French settlers in Wisconsin.

Vilatte was independent-minded to the point of being stubborn, and did not take well to the efforts of the Episcopal Church to assert increasing authority over his missions. He contacted a number of different churches, hoping for help. Eventually, he found himself in lively correspondence with Mar Julius I (Antonio Alvarez), a bishop in Ceylon (Sri Lanka) who was in communion with the Syrian Orthodox Church. In 1892, Vilatte journeyed to Ceylon and was consecrated as a bishop by Alvarez.

Much like Arnold Mathew, Vilatte quickly began ordaining and consecrating a wide variety of men for various missions. Most famously, he consecrated a former Episcopal priest, George Alexander McGuire, who had left the white-dominated Episcopal Church under the influence of Marcus Garvey's ideas. McGuire founded a significant African-American denomination, the African Orthodox Church, which continues to the present.

Vilatte spent his final years, from 1925 until his death in 1929, living in a cottage on the grounds of a Roman Catholic Cistercian abbey near Versailles, France. While he was, in theory, now a layman in submission to Rome, he began celebrating mass in his cottage, and possibly acting as a priest in other ways. Along with Arnold Mathew, he is one of the two most important ancestors of the contemporary Independent movement.

herford and other eastern ancestors

Some Independent Catholic ancestors such as Vilatte were probably quite difficult and willful people. Perhaps such strong personalities were needed for people who were striving to chart a new way forward. But, like all branches of Christianity, through the grace of the Spirit, we also have our saints.

One of our most saintly ancestors is Ulric Vernon Herford. Herford was a minister in a branch of the Unitarian movement which described itself as Liberal Christianity. He wanted to find a liturgical, Catholic tradition for Liberal Christians. In 1903, he traveled to India and was consecrated as bishop by Luis Mariano Suares, a bishop of the Assyrian Church of the East, a very ancient Eastern church with roots in the 5th century. He was later consecrated again by a bishop with lineage running back to the Roman Church.

Returning home to England, Herford became a tireless worker for pacifism, animal welfare, and a wide array of social causes. The generally disheveled bishop was often seen bicycling around Oxford, promoting the betterment of all creatures, before returning home to his patient Anglican wife and large herd of cats. Even his detractors noted his sincerity and kindness.

Another important spiritual ancestor (also considered a saint by some) from the Eastern churches is Bishop Aftimios Ofiesh, a Syrian priest consecrated by the Russian church, with the intent of creating a fully American, English-speaking Orthodox jurisdiction. Largely as a result of the fighting among ethnic Orthodox jurisdictions, compounded by pressure from the Episcopal Church, which did not welcome potential competition from western rite Orthodoxy, the Russian church withdrew support from Ofiesh in 1929. Nonetheless, he continued onward with his American mission, which has survived to the present in a number of groups.

There are many other minor sources of independent holy orders from the Christian east, ranging from Ethiopian missionaries, to various Russians stranded by political changes in their homeland, to stray Cypriots and Albanians, to an assortment of Greek Old Calendrists. There are also claims emanating from the Melkite and Chaldean rites of the Roman Catholic Church. It would take us beyond our limitations of space to sort out this history, although it makes for fascinating reading, if you wish to explore further. (See Appendix 2, "Further Reading," on p. 72 for some suggestions.)

anglican roots and branches

Despite the doubts regarding the validity of the Anglican priesthood, which provided an impetus for the spread of Old Catholicism, the Anglican Communion has made its own contributions to the ancestry of today's Independent Catholic jurisdictions. The first significant case is that of the Reformed Episcopal Church. George Cummins was a former Methodist circuit rider who had become the assistant bishop of Kentucky in the Episcopal Church. Dismayed by the increasing power of the Anglo-Catholic movement, and in trouble for presiding over an ecumenical Eucharist including ministers not ordained in apostolic succession, Cummins resigned his position in 1873, and organized the Reformed Episcopal Church. The REC has continued to represent a very conservative, evangelical, low church Anglicanism, preserving apostolic succession, but with more stress upon apostolic doctrine. Largely by way of REC missions to Puerto Rico and England, its claim to the historic episcopate has been inherited by many Independent communities.

There are also a number of other connections to Anglican ancestry. William Montgomery Brown was the Episcopal Bishop of Arkansas in the early 20th century. In 1924, he was excommunicated for his interest in the ideas of Darwin and Marx, among others. For a number of years afterwards, Brown functioned as an independent bishop. On the other side of the world, in the Philippines, some clergy and laypeople had left the Roman Catholic Church in 1902 over political and ethnic troubles. In 1948, bishops from the Episcopal Church consecrated bishops for the Philippine Independent Church, some of which later forged ties with the Independent movement.

More recently, we have seen the rise of the "Continuing Anglican" movement in North America, among conservatives from the Episcopal Church. These traditionalists have formed independent jurisdictions with holy orders provided by current or former bishops of the Episcopal Church. The first such consecration was that of four bishops for the Anglican Church in North America on January 28, 1978. The primary consecrator was Albert A. Chambers, retired Bishop of Springfield in the Episcopal Church. Other similar events have followed, and, with the unfortunate divisions in the Episcopal Church, seem likely to continue.

other roman roots

The last century has also seen a number of departures from the Roman Church, some including bishops who, directly or indirectly, contributed to the history of the Independent Catholic movement. Perhaps the largest departure from the Roman Catholic Church in recent times was that of the Czechoslovak Hussite Church. This liberal schism, consisting of several thousand priests and laypeople, was organized in 1920 and eventually received apostolic succession through a bishop with lineage from Arnold Mathew. It is a large church in Europe, but has had little impact in North America.

Another relatively large schism was that led by Bishop Carlos Duarte Costa in Brazil. Bishop Duarte Costa was openly critical of Vatican policies on clerical celibacy, divorce, vernacular liturgy, and other matters. He advocated for liberal social issues, such as land reform, and denounced Catholic clergy who were fascist sympathizers during World War II. As a result, he had trouble with the authorities in Brazil, and was excommunicated by Rome in 1945. He founded the Brazilian Catholic Apostolic Church, which remains sizeable in Brazil and has many descendents in North America.

Since the exit of the Brazilian Catholics, the most important schisms from the Roman Church have been related to traditionalists, who oppose some or all of the reforms of the Second Vatican Council, and who may or may not regard the current pope as legitimate. By far the most famous traditionalist Roman prelate of recent times is the late French Archbishop Marcel Lefebvre, who founded the Society of St. Pius X in 1970 and was excommunicated by Rome in 1988. However, there are a number of other, similar traditionalist groups, which mostly keep their distance from their Independent Catholic cousins.

new priesthoods

Our consideration of Independent Catholic history would not be complete without some acknowledgement of new priesthoods, allegedly founded through spiritual inspiration, without a hands-on-heads connection to historic apostolic succession. Jurisdictions which have new priesthoods often appear all but identical in every other way to Independent Catholic jurisdictions.

Some groups with a new priesthood, such as the Evangelical Orthodox Church in the United States and the Christengemeinschaft in Germany, have never acquired historic succession. (Part of the Evangelical Orthodox Church joined the Antiochian Orthodox Church some years ago, but another portion continues as an independent jurisdiction.) Other groups, such as many of the descendents of the new priesthoods founded by Jules Doinel and Paul Blighton, have later blended their spiritual inheritance with traditional apostolic succession.

conclusion

The Independent Catholic movement has an incredibly diverse heritage, inherited from the historic churches of east and west, and even from several new priesthoods inaugurated in the last two hundred years. Due to mergers and prolific cross-fertilization, many jurisdictions you may encounter will have ancestry from most of the sources discussed above. With such an extensive ancestry, each contemporary group makes its own choices of emphasis in terms of doctrine, liturgy, and other matters. We will now turn to a consideration of the "brands and flavors" of independent jurisdictions found in the United States today.

3 • brands and flavors

THE INDEPENDENT CATHOLIC MOVEMENT, and other closely related groups, come in an incredibly diverse number of "flavors," which can prove both exciting and bewildering to the new inquirer. The freedom inherent in the movement guarantees that someone is always creating a new version. It is also not uncommon to find clergy, lay members, and even whole communities which migrate over time from one jurisdiction to another, in response to their unique spiritual journeys. In a short book such as this, we cannot begin to cover the full spectrum of theological and liturgical diversity in the movement, but we can introduce you to several of the major "families" which you are likely to encounter.

liberal

If you glance on the internet or in the phone book, the largest group of jurisdictions falls under a category which we can describe as "Liberal." By this, we indicate churches which are carrying forward a spirit of inclusivity and dialogue with modern thought within a sacramental, Catholic context.

Such communities usually draw upon the post-Vatican II liturgy of the Roman Catholic Church, and/or the liturgies of the Episcopal Church's *Book of Common Prayer.* There is often a warm intimacy and an emphasis on community participation in the liturgy. The setting is often very relaxed. In smaller communities, the altar may be a coffee table or dining room table, with everyone gathered around. Communion is usually open to all baptized Christians, and sometimes even to the non-baptized who are drawn to Christ in the sacrament.

Most liberal communities will welcome women in ordained ministry, and encourage the full inclusion of gay, lesbian, bisexual, and transgendered persons. Some groups will do blessings or marriages for same-sex couples. The traditional creeds are often used, but with an explicit emphasis on freedom of theological interpretation. Alternative language for God (feminine or gender-neutral) may be used. Liberal communities may also incorporate elements drawn from non-Catholic sources. For example, I (John P.) was once a part of a community which borrowed silent worship and consensus decision-making from the Religious Society of Friends (Quakers).

If you are comfortable with the liturgy in the contemporary Roman and Episcopal churches, but long for a greater degree of inclusivity and theological flexibility, a liberal Independent Catholic community may be just the place for you! These welcoming and open churches form the fastest-growing part of the movement.

traditionalists

At the other end of the spectrum, we find the traditionalist groups. Some traditionalists are Catholics who want to celebrate the pre-Vatican II, Tridentine rite (often in Latin), some are Continuing Anglicans who are devoted to the 1928 *Book of Common Prayer*, and some are Orthodox with a commitment to particularly strict adherence to the details of Orthodox liturgy (and often the use of the old, Julian calendar). The actor Mel Gibson has recently drawn attention to this end of the movement, due to his membership in a Tridentine rite independent community.

Traditionalist communities are more likely than liberals to have a formal chapel or building, as their liturgies are less flexible and portable, and require more equipment. Worship tends to be more formal, and the priest will usually be facing East (toward the altar). Visitors will be made welcome, but you may need to ask a member of the community to help you figure out what to do (sit, stand, kneel, gestures, etc.) at various points in the complex but beautiful liturgies. In many traditionalist communities, communion may be closed to non-members. You should be sure to ask what the community's policy is before going forward for communion. The community will be grateful for your respect.

The majority of traditionalist groups have a very conservative theology. However, this is not always the case. As you navigate through the Independent Catholic movement, you will discover that conservative liturgy does not always accompany conservative theology, and vice versa. For example, you might find a group with a liberal, post-Vatican II liturgy, and an inclusive membership, but a very conservative interpretation of the creeds and charismatic speaking in tongues. Likewise, it is entirely possible to have a highly traditionalist liturgy, but to ordain women or be open to gay and lesbian people. I recall a Latin language, Tridentine rite parish which opposed women's ordination, and yet met in a gay community center with a pastor who would conduct same-sex marriages. Surprises lurk around every corner, which underscores the need to ask lots of questions!

esoteric

If you are coming from a mainstream church background, one of the most unusual flavors in the Independent movement will be esotericism. These churches may also be referred to as metaphysical, occult, or Gnostic. These words can sound very scary and heretical if you are not familiar with these groups. On the other hand, if you are coming from a New Age or alternative religious background, you may be relieved to discover esoteric communities!

The word esoteric simply means "inner," occult means "hidden," and metaphysical is "beyond the physical." Gnostic comes from the Greek word for knowledge, and refers to an inner, spiritual knowledge of the Divine. As you can gather from these terms, the esoteric communities have a focus on inner spiritual processes, and often look at the sacraments as an alchemical process of inner transformation, or initiation into a deeper experience of God.

Esotericism, or an inner approach to Christianity, has been a part of the Independent movement for a long time. A Frenchman named Jules Doinel founded an esoteric sacramental church, L'Eglise Gnostique, in France in the late 19th century. And in the early 20th century, some members of the esoterically-oriented Theosophical Society founded the Liberal Catholic Church. The vast majority of contemporary metaphysical churches have been influenced, to some degree, by one or both of these groups.

An esoteric community may have a fairly traditional liturgy and theology, but a more meditative approach, and an interest in symbols and inner (psychic, spiritual, visionary) dynamics. On the other hand, such a group may be highly idiosyncratic, with unique teachings and liturgical practices arising from the spiritual experiences of the members. Here again, asking is everything! Some esoteric churches are private, but most are open to visitors and inclusive in membership. Words and concepts (such as Christ, the Trinity, etc.) may be used with different meanings than those to which you are accustomed, so listen carefully and inquire liberally. Any sane and balanced esoteric church will be happy to explain its beliefs and practices. An unwillingness to be forthcoming and to answer questions in a clear way should be taken as a warning sign.

If you are disturbed by phenomena like the New Age, magic, and alternative religions, you will probably not find the esoteric communities to be a good fit for you. But if you have a background in these matters, and are looking for a way to integrate your interests and practices with Christianity and the sacramental life, the esoteric communities will have much to offer.

syncretistic & others

Some Independent Catholic communities defy easy classification as liberal, traditional, or esoteric, and may combine features of all three. They may incorporate influences from other parts of the Christian tradition (evangelical, charismatic, Quaker, Methodist, etc.). Some communities also reach beyond Christianity. Sometimes this means simply adding a time of Zen-based meditation. Other times, the influence is more profound. I (John P.) am familiar with an Independent community which has been strongly influenced by neo-pagan approaches to the Divine Feminine, and has made use of this material theologically and liturgically. Another group I have been privileged to meet combines a Russian Orthodox spirituality with Siberian/Mongolian shamanism, and Tendai and Shingon Buddhism, resulting in a very interesting spiritual synthesis.

Like St. Paul, the Independent Catholic movement has great potential to be all things to all people. Initially, you might see this as a confusing mess. And it is always possible to identify communities which are unhealthy or just plain weird. But we would suggest to you that it is actually the Spirit at work, creating a diversity of communities to meet the spiritual needs of an immense variety of unique human beings. There is a place for everyone who is drawn toward the Catholic tradition—and in the Independent movement, there is no need for anyone to compromise their identity or spiritual integrity to find a home.

4 • care and handling
of independent catholic clergy

OFTEN, THE FIRST THING OUT of people's mouths when they meet me is, "So what do I call you—'*Father*'?" I usually smile and tell them that they may call me anything, so long as it is kind!

"My parishioners call me 'Father,' yes," I usually continue, "but you can just call me 'John' if you feel more comfortable with that." A lot of the people I serve are not Catholics, and so calling someone they have never met before "Father" is simply not natural for them! They often have a lot of questions about what seem to me to be normal, simple interactions, but are unsure about how to proceed.

This is not unusual. People are often very nervous when they first meet clergy, and I am keenly aware that not everyone has had positive experiences with the clergy. Some people have just never been around us and do not know the "protocol." In this chapter we'll take a look at what you need to know—and what you can do—to make your interactions with an Independent Catholic clergyperson a positive experience for everyone involved.

finding an independent catholic church

Because Independents often do not have buildings to house their ministries, they are not as visible as clergy of the larger churches. Nevertheless, we are a numerous lot and can be found with just a little searching. The *Yellow Pages* is a good place to start, as many Independent parishes have listings. Just look for those "Catholic," "Anglican," "Orthodox," or "Sacramental" ministries that appear different from the larger churches that use those same names (usually distinguished by adding another word to modify the classification, such as "Apostolic Catholic Church," or "American Orthodox," or "Charismatic Episcopal Church," or "United Anglican," or any number of other combinations).

Most Independent jurisdictions maintain a website of some sort. You can find links to numerous Independent churches at www.ind-movement.org and www.concentric.net/~cosmas/ficob.htm among many others. (Please keep in mind the ephemeral nature of web pages—some of the links on these sites are already out of date, and more will be by the time you read this.)

When exploring a jurisdiction's website or talking to someone on the phone (if you've called from the phone book), it is a good idea to see if the "charism" or "personality" of the jurisdiction is a good fit for you. As we saw in our last chapter, there are many "brands" and "flavors" of Independent Catholic jurisdictions, and it will be very important to find one that is "on the same page" as you are. For instance, if you consider yourself to be pretty conservative, theologically, it would be best to find a jurisdiction that has the same basic orientation. Calling a liberal jurisdiction may land you with someone that is simply not a good fit, especially if you do not approve of women priests or gay clergy.

Similarly, if your spirituality is eclectic (or even New Age), a priest from a Traditional jurisdiction will probably not be able to give you exactly what you need. A Liberal or an Esoteric jurisdiction will probably be a better fit. The front page of a jurisdiction's website may not give a clear indication of the jurisdiction's "personality," as even Liberal and Esoteric jurisdictions have a fondness for traditional iconography and language. Poking around the innards of the site will give you a better idea. Read the "What We Believe" page or even a few posted sermons to get a better idea.

Likewise, if you are talking to someone on the phone, do not be shy. Everyone concerned will be grateful to have all the cards on the table. It is not fair to you or to a clergyperson to wait until he or she has put in several hours of meetings before you explore the issue of basic compatibility (although you will probably have a good idea by that time, anyway). Simple questions like, "How would you describe your church? Do you take a conservative or liberal approach to things? Are you open to working with someone who is *(insert your own spiritual approach here)*?" Nobody will take offense, and it may save everyone a lot of time and trouble.

selecting an
independent catholic clergyperson

Once you have found a jurisdiction or church that seems like a good fit for your own spirituality, it is time to interview a clergyperson. Some people are content to simply talk on the phone, but I strongly discourage this. It is very important to meet with a deacon, priest, or bishop face-to-face in order to evaluate them properly. Unfortunately, circumstances do not always permit this, and sometimes you just have to go on faith. Nevertheless, it is always preferable to meet with them personally.

I (John M.) usually invite couples who are considering me for their wedding out for breakfast or dinner. For baptisms, usually the whole family comes along. This provides a neutral meeting place, and also a social context to get to know each other as people. Other clergy prefer to meet people in their homes or offices. If you have a preference, let the priest you are meeting with know.

When you go to meet with clergy people, try not to be nervous or shy. After all, they are not so much interviewing you as you are interviewing them. They are not there to judge you or your spirituality or your lifestyle or your ideas. They are there to serve you, *period.* And *you* get to say whether they are appropriate for your needs or not.

Remember that the clergy people you meet are just people. They brush their teeth and go to the bathroom and scrub tile grout and pick up after the dog just like you do. They have no elevated status, and they have no authority over you whatsoever. Undue awe left over from childhood church experiences are not necessary—you may leave that kind of baggage at home. For best results, treat them just as you would like to be treated yourself: with respect, kindness, and consideration.

You might begin by telling the clergyperson what it is you are looking for. If he or she is uncomfortable with what you propose, or considers it a bad fit, he or she will tell you so. Don't worry if you find you need to interview more than one clergyperson to find just the right fit.

If your clergyperson seems fine with what you propose, he or she may ask you some more questions about yourself or your spiritual approach. Again, this is no time for inappropriate awe. Don't adjust your answers according to what you think the clergyperson wants to hear. Be brutally honest, and say exactly what you think. You will not shock anyone, or hurt anyone's feelings. If your clergyperson gets up and walks off in a huff, consider yourself lucky that you wasted no more time on him or her! Most likely, this will not happen. Honesty is always the best policy, and this is especially true when it comes to spiritual or religious issues.

When you feel the time is right, ask whatever questions you might have about the clergyperson. You might ask questions like: "What is your ministry like?" "How much experience do you have conducting weddings / performing baptisms / conducting memorial services (or whatever else you are interviewing him or her about)?" "Where did you go to school?" and "Can you describe your personal spirituality?" Most clergy will be happy to talk about any of these questions—perhaps at greater length than you actually want to hear! Don't be afraid to put up your hand and say, "Okay, I get the idea...." and go on to your next question. One thing most clergy love to do is talk!

remuneration

Invariably, at some point during our meeting someone will ask me, "What do you charge?" This is a very tricky issue for clergy, for a number of reasons. First of all, theologically, we are not permitted to charge money for sacraments. This is the sin of simony, and all clergy are wise to avoid it. Another sensitive area is that most clergy represent non-profit organizations and cannot charge for services at risk of endangering the non-profit status of their parish or jurisdiction.

Nevertheless, your clergyperson is a professional, and must pay his or her bills just like everyone else. It may be a sin to charge for a sacrament, but it is equally wrong to take advantage of a clergyperson.

Remember that his or her time is just as valuable as yours is, and some compensation is only fair. A fair donation in gratitude for your clergyperson's time is most appropriate.

Most jurisdictions have some official guidelines for suggested donations. For instance, I (John M.) am associated with a network of Bay Area clergy that recommends a donation of $450 for weddings in my own immediate area. If I have to drive between twenty-five and fifty miles, $550 is recommended. The amount is increased further for longer drives.

If you are planning a wedding, and your clergy person does not have a guideline to give you, you can easily figure out a fair amount for yourself. Taking into account that your clergyperson has one preliminary meeting with you, is present at the rehearsal and at the wedding itself, of course, and including travel time and whatever time he or she spends preparing the liturgy, it is fair to assume that he or she will be putting in ten to twelve hours on your wedding. Think of what your personal hourly wage is, and pay him or her what you yourself would expect to make in ten or twelve hours at your own job.

This is a kind of sliding scale that most clergy can support. On the other hand, it may be that you are really and truly impoverished, and you can afford no more than a token offering, or perhaps even nothing. If this is the case, be up-front about this with your clergy person. He or she will still perform the sacrament for you (if not, he or she should probably not be in ordained ministry), but there will be no misunderstandings or hard feelings when there is no offering (or too small an offering) made later.

appropriate caution

Just as with clergy of all jurisdictions, there are a few Independent Catholic priests who do not behave ethically. The Roman Catholic Church has been wracked by the clergy abuse scandal, and Protestant denominations have had their own—albeit less publicized—struggles with clergy misconduct. It would be dishonest to portray all Independent Catholic clergy as being somehow beyond occasional indiscretions. Independent Catholic clergy are just as human and fallible as the clergy of any other churches, and just like other clergy, every barrel has some bad apples.

That is why it is important to carefully interview your clergyperson. Because Independent Catholic jurisdictions vary widely in their formation practices, many of them do not require their clergy to undergo the same degree of psychological testing that the larger churches insist upon. Also, many jurisdictions do their own education and training, and these are sometimes not as rigorous as the seminary programs of the larger churches.

This does not mean that Independent Catholic clergy are in any way inferior to the clergy of the larger churches. Indeed, I have met many excellent deacons, priests, and bishops in the Independent movement, each of whom are in every way the equal of, and often superior to, many clergy I have met from the larger churches. On the other hand, I have also met some Independent clergy who are, to put it kindly, fairly eccentric folk whom I would not trust to baptize my cat.

Due caution must be observed when dealing with professionals in any sphere, and clergy are no different. Just because someone has the endorsement of the Roman Catholic Church or the Episcopal Church does not necessarily make him or her moral or even competent. Likewise, just because a person is from an Independent jurisdiction does not make him or her in any way suspect. Independent Catholic clergy have been honorably serving God's people for hundreds of years, and usually to the people's great satisfaction. The great majority of us are sincere and compassionate pastors who endeavor with everything that is in us to carry this legacy of responsible service on into the future.

If you feel that the clergy person you have contracted with has in any way disappointed you or breached what would be widely considered to be ethical conduct, do not hesitate to report your feelings to his or her bishop. It is the bishop's job to make sure his or her clergy are behaving responsibly and ethically, and he or she will be very grateful for the feedback. You must remember that you are not the only person this clergyperson will serve, and if you have experienced trouble, others most likely will, too. You owe it to yourself and to those who will come after you to report any unprofessional behavior to the bishop.

a kind word is always welcome

If you are happy with the service your clergy person has rendered—be it a wedding, a baptism, a funeral, or some pastoral counseling—why not send him or her a little note expressing your thanks? A kind word is always welcome, and it will mean a great deal to Independent Catholic clergy, who often do not see the people they serve again after the sacrament has been performed.

But there is no reason to be a stranger. If you really hit it off with your clergyperson, why not drop in for Mass or a healing service sometime? It might be that you could find a home in Independent Catholicism when you didn't even know you were looking for it.

Many Independent clergy become "family ministers" without even intending to. I can't count how many times I have performed a wedding for a couple, who then call me about a year later for a baptism. Then another year later, Uncle Tom is getting married, and would I do that one as well? So who knows? Perhaps your initial encounter with your clergyperson will not be your last.

appendices

appendix 1
old catholic beliefs in comparison with roman catholic and protestant beliefs

THIS CHART IS INSPIRED by and very loosely based on one found in *Précis d'histoire de l'Englise* by Urs Küry, published by the *Catholiques-chrétiennes* (Christian Catholics/Old Catholics in Switzerland), 1968. Because of the broad theological spectrum found in Independent Catholicism, this should not be taken as a statement of the beliefs of the movement as a whole. It is, however, an accurate representation of the beliefs of the European Old Catholics from which most Independent Catholics in the United States are, at least in part, descended, and is representative of beliefs commonly found in US Independent Catholic communities. Orthodox Christians would be in agreement with most Roman Catholic positions, while Anglicans (a category which includes Episcopalians in the United States) which are technically both Catholic *and* Protestant, would be in general agreement with the Old Catholic positions on most of the items below.

sources of revelation

Roman Catholic: Scripture and Catholic Tradition

Old Catholic: same

Protestant: Scripture alone.

scripture

Roman Catholic: The scriptures were written by human beings, under the inspiration of the Holy Spirit, the proper interpretation of which is safeguarded by the Church.

Old Catholic: same

Protestant: The scriptures were written by human beings, under the inspiration of the Holy Spirit. Some Protestants believe that correct interpretation is a matter between the individual believer and God.

tradition

Roman Catholic: Catholic Tradition explains the scriptures and completes them. It continues to develop under the guidance of the Holy Spirit.

Old Catholic: Catholic Tradition helps explain the scriptures, and although its development has been guided by the Holy Spirit, it has not done so infallibly. Tradition contains errors, and Old Catholics continue to seek God's will in understanding and reforming tradition.

Protestant: Some Protestants would agree with the Old Catholic assessment, but most would agree that Tradition is in no way binding upon believers.

correct teaching

Roman Catholic: The Church's teaching is decided through the Supreme Magisterium of the Papal office. The Pope alone makes final decisions as to what is essential to Catholic teaching and practice, and he may designate certain of his decisions "infallible."

Old Catholic: Correct teaching is discerned through general councils, with various regional churches represented by their bishops.

Protestant: Most Protestant churches discern doctrine by decision of regional councils of democratically elected representatives, some of whom are clergy, and some lay. While the decisions of these councils may be final for official declarations, it is expected that individual believers ultimately follow their consciences.

expressions of correct doctrine

Roman Catholic: Accepts the decisions of the first seven ecumenical councils, and adds to them the decisions made at fourteen additional councils, including the First and Second Vatican Councils.

Old Catholic: Accepts the decisions of the first seven ecumenical councils.

Protestant: Each denomination generally issues one or more confessions of faith. The Lutherans, for instance, hold to the *Augsburg Confession,* and Reformed hold to the *Westminster Confession of Faith.* Even Southern Baptists, tradition-ally a non-creedal and non-confessional denomination, have issued an official statement in *The Baptist Faith and Message.*

Orthodox, like Old Catholics, accept only the first seven councils.

the church

Roman Catholic: The Church is that body of people, living and dead, who confessed the One faith, have participated in its sacraments, and have submitted to the authority of the hierarchy. Under the teachings of Vatican II, non-Romans and even non-Christians may, in fact, be saved at God's discretion.

Old Catholic: The Church is that body of people, living and dead, who confessed the One faith, have participated in its sacraments, and have remained faithful to the essential teachings of the historical church.

Protestant: The Church consists of all those who have been made one Body in Christ by the Holy Spirit, evidenced by confessing the faith, acknowledging of the authority of Scripture, and faithfully following Christ in Baptism.

the ministry

Roman Catholic: Christ himself ordained the apostles and sent them forth to minister to the world. The laity receive the general priesthood and are responsible for ministering the grace of Jesus Christ in their homes and workplaces. The ordained ministry consists of deacons, priests, and bishops, who have received a sacrament by the Holy Spirit through the laying on of hands in unbroken succession all the way back to Jesus, and these have a special responsibility for the spiritual health of the laity and the propagation of the Gospel.

Old Catholic: *same*

Protestant: Ministers are called by the Holy Spirit and ordained by the laying on of hands. This ceremony is not a sacrament that transmits grace, but is a public witness of the trust placed in an individual by the worshipping community.

the pope

Roman Catholic: The papacy was founded by Christ, and continues to speak with the authority of Peter, the Rock of the Church and the first Pope. The Pope speaks with absolute authority over the whole Christian church (including those "separated brethren," whether they accept his authority or not), and can designate certain teachings as infallible.

Old Catholic: The Pope is the *primus inter pares,* the first bishop among equals, and has the right to be the official spokesman for the whole Christian church, in much the same way as the Ecumenical Patriarch is the first among equals for the Orthodox Communion. In the same way the Archbishop of Utrecht is the first among equals for the Old Catholic communion and the Archbishop of Canterbury has the same role for Anglicans. However, the Pope, like the Archbishops of Utrecht and Canterbury, should not have any official authority over national churches, which are autonomous and joined together in voluntary communion.

Protestant: The Pope has no authority whatsoever. The Papacy is a human institution which has unjustly imposed itself upon the church.

Orthodox Christians agree with the Old Catholic position on this matter.

salvation

Roman Catholic: Through the infinite merits of Jesus Christ, won by him through his sacrifice, a gift of infinite grace has been bestowed upon him, which is measured out to those who avail themselves of it through union with the One Church and participation in its sacraments. Through his efforts and his grace, humankind is saved from sin and justified before God. By participation in the sacramental life of the church and through works of mercy believers are sanctified and grow in the life of the Holy Spirit.

Old Catholic: The crucifixion and resurrection of Jesus Christ liberate us from sin and allow us to enter into full union with God, which we do in practice by uniting with and participating in the life of the Church. Through the guidance of the Holy Spirit, we learn to cooperate with God's will, growing spiritually, and exhibiting this growth outwardly through works of mercy.

Protestant: We are saved by grace alone through faith in Jesus Christ. Church attendance is helpful for one's spiritual growth, but not necessary for salvation, which is deemed an affair between God and the individual soul. Spiritual growth comes through study of the Scriptures and is evidenced through works of mercy and deeper understanding of scriptural teaching.

the eucharist

Roman Catholic: Through it believers not only relive Jesus' offering of himself in history, but see it enacted in the flesh before their very eyes. Through the miracle of transubstantiation, the bread and wine become the actual, historical body and blood of Jesus Christ. When consumed by the faithful, they both physically and mystically join themselves to the Body of Christ.

Old Catholic: Through it believers re-enact the once-and-for-all historical sacrifice of Christ. After consecration, the bread and wine contain the real presence of Christ, which, when consumed by the faithful, mystically joins them to his Body.

Protestant: Lutherans would agree with the Old Catholics on this one, but other Protestants simply see it as a symbolic memorial of Christ's sacrifice. Christ is present not in the bread and wine, but in the gathered community through the Holy Spirit.

penance

Roman Catholic: Roman Catholics liturgically employ a general confession, but also require individual confession before one can participate in the Eucharist. Confession of one's sins to a priest is a sacrament, which is complete when a person has performed the prescribed penance for his or her sins.

Old Catholic: Old Catholics employ a general confession and absolution in the liturgy, which, when done in the presence of a priest, suffices to absolve the people of their sins. For grave sins, individuals may make an appointment with a priest for private confession, of which pastoral counseling is also an important component. Both public and private confessions are seen as sacramentally efficacious.

Protestant: Many Protestants use a general confession liturgically, but most do not see it as a sacrament. Confession is usually seen as a private matter between the individual and God, not requiring the mediation of a clergyperson.

the last judgment

Roman Catholic: Unrepentent souls immediately enter a miserable state void of God's presence, otherwise known as Hell. Believers go to Purgatory, where they are purified of their sins before being admitted into Heaven. Only saints and martyrs go directly to Heaven. At the general resurrection, the soul will be reunited with the body.

Old Catholic: Souls enter an intermediate state in anticipation of the ultimate return of Christ, where they are purified by God's grace. Those who are unrepentant will experience this state as extremely uncomfortable, while the faithful will experience it as pleasurable. At the end of time,

Christ will judge the living and the dead. The faithful will enter into eternal bliss. The fate of unbelievers is a matter of some disagreement amongst Old Catholics, some of whom believe in an eternal Hell, and some of whom do not.

Protestant: Some Protestants, such as Seventh Day Adventists, believe that the dead await Christ's return in an intermediate state, but most Protestants teach that believers enter immediately into the joys of Heaven at death, and that the unrepentant enter immediately into Hell.

veneration of saints

Roman Catholic: All Christians are saints, but some are marked by a specific degree of holiness that is worthy of respect and the celebration of their memory. Saints may be prayed to in order to solicit their intercession, and also for the fulfillment of special requests, as most canonized saints have specialized areas of concern and assistance.

Old Catholic: All Christians are saints, but some are marked by a specific degree of holiness that is worthy of respect and the celebration of their memory. Saints may be prayed to in order to solicit their intercession.

Protestant: All Christians are saints, and none are held as more venerable than any other. The dead are not to be prayed to, as prayer as seen as being synonymous with worship, which must be reserved for God alone.

It must be noted that for Catholics, prayer to saints is not the same as worship of saints. In Catholic tradition "praying to" and "worship of" should not be confused. Praying to a saint is simply talking to someone who is not physically present. Asking a saint to pray for you is essentially no different than calling a friend on the telephone and soliciting their prayers for a specific concern. Neither the saint nor the friend on the phone are physically present, and neither are being worshipped.

mary

Roman Catholic: Mary is an especially important saint, worthy of special veneration. She is believed to have been born without original sin (known as the Immaculate Conception) and to have been bodily assumed into heaven. She was perpetually a virgin, and is the Virgin Mother of God. She alone has the status of co-redemptrix, because the redeeming work of Christ would have been impossible without her.

Old Catholic: Mary is an important saint, and worthy of special veneration. She was a virgin when she gave birth to Jesus.

Protestant: Mary was a virgin when she gave birth to Jesus and is seen as a model of obedience and Christian motherhood. She is respected but not venerated.

sacraments

Roman Catholic: A sacrament is an outward and visible sign of the real but invisible grace of God. Through the sacraments we can be certain that we have received grace, because they are efficacious on their own merits (*ex epere operato*).

Old Catholic: A sacrament is an outward and visible sign of the real but invisible grace of God. They are efficacious according to the degree of our faith in them.

Protestant: Protestants differ markedly in their understanding of the nature of the sacraments. Mostly they are simply seen as symbols of inward realities, representing those realities but not conferring them, although Lutherans are closer to the Old Catholic position.

names of the sacraments

Roman Catholic: Baptism, Confirmation, Eucharist, Confession, Holy Orders, Marriage, Unction (Anointing of the Sick and Last Rites).

Old Catholic: same

Protestant: Most mainline Protestants honor Baptism and Eucharist as the only sacraments. Most Free Church Protestants reject the notion of sacraments altogether and may practice Baptism and the Lord's Supper as "ordinances."

baptism

Roman Catholic: Since we are saved as a Church and not as individuals, Baptism welcomes the child or the baptized adult onto the "ark" of the church, removes any taint of inherited or earned guilt, and bestows upon him or her the fullness of salvation promised to members of Christ's body.

Old Catholic:　　same

Protestant:　　Some Protestants baptize infants to remove original sin and welcome them into the community of the church. Others accept only the baptism of adults, which is not in any way efficacious, but merely an outward symbol of the believer's inward transformation wrought by the Holy Spirit.

Orthodox Christians distinguish between Western and Eastern notions of "original sin." In the Western Church, largely through the influence of St. Augustine, people are believed to be born with a stain of guilt inherited from Adam. Eastern Christians believe babies are born with a clean slate, but are quickly poisoned by the "original sin" inherent in human society and invariably taught to the child by all-too-human parents and their communities.

appendix 2
further reading

dutch old catholic history

Moss, C.B. *The Old Catholic Movement* (London: Society for Promoting Christian Knowledge, 1948; reprinted by the Apocryphile Press, 2005).

Neale, John M. *History of the So-Called Jansenist Church of Holland* (John Hentry and James Parker, 1858; reprinted by the Apocryphile Press, 2005).

independent catholic history

Anson, Peter. *Bishops at Large* (London: Faber and Faber, 1964; reprinted by the Apocryphile Press, 2006).

Brandreth, H.R.T. *Episcopi Vagantes and the Anglican Church* (London: Society for Promoting Christian Knowledge, 1947; reprinted by the Apocryphile Press, 2006).

Newman-Norton, Seraphim. *Flesh of Our Brethren* (British Orthodox Press, 2006).

Plummer, John P. *The Many Paths of the Independent Sacramental Movement* (Newt Books, 2005; reprinted by the Apocryphile Press, 2006).

Pruter, Karl. *The Old Catholic Church: A History and Chronology* (St. Willibrord's Press; 2nd edition, December 1996).

Pruter, Karl and J. Gordon Melton. *The Old Catholic Sourcebook* (Taylor and Francis, 1983).

Ward, Gary L., Bertil Persson, and Alan Bain. *Independent Bishops: An International Directory* (Omnigraphics, 1990).

traditionalist jurisdictions

Bess, Douglas. *Divided We Stand: A History of the Continuing Anglican Movement* (Tractarian Press, 2002; reprinted by the Apocryphile Press, 2006).

Cuneo, Michael. *The Smoke of Satan: Conservative and Traditionalist Dissent in Contemporary American Catholicism* (John Hopkins University Press, 1999).

appendix 3
historical documents

apostle's creed

I BELIEVE IN GOD the Father almighty; maker of heaven and earth; and in Jesus Christ his only son our Lord; who was conceived by the Holy Spirit, born of the virgin Mary; suffered under Pontius Pilate, was crucified, dead, and buried; he descended into Hell. The third day he rose again from the dead: he ascended into Heaven, and sitteth on the right hand of God, the Father almighty. From thence he shall come to judge the quick and the dead. I believe in the Holy Spirit; the holy Catholic Church; the communion of saints; the forgiveness of sins; the resurrection of the body; and the life everlasting. Amen.

nicene creed

I BELIEVE IN ONE GOD, the Father, the Almighty, maker of heaven and earth, of all that is, seen and unseen. I believe in one Lord, Jesus Christ, the only Son of God, eternally begotten of the Father, God from God, light from light, true God from true God, begotten, not made, of one being with the Father. Through him all things were made. For us and for our salvation he came down from heaven: by the power of the Holy Spirit he became incarnate from the virgin Mary, and was made man. For our sake he was crucified under Pontius Pilate; he suffered death and was buried. On the third day he rose again in accordance with the scriptures; he ascended into heaven and is seated at the right hand of the Father. He will come again in glory to judge the living and the dead, and his kingdom will have no end. We believe in the Holy Spirit, the Lord, the giver of life, who proceeds from the Father [and the Son]. With the Father and the Son he is worshiped and glorified. He has spoken through the prophets. I believe in one holy Catholic and apostolic Church. I acknowledge one baptism for the forgiveness of sins. I look for the resurrection of the dead, and the life of the world to come. Amen.

declaration of the catholic congress at munich—september 22-24, 1871

1. CONSCIOUS OF OUR RELIGIOUS DUTIES, we hold fast to the Old Catholic creed and worship, as attested in scripture, and in tradition. We regard ourselves, therefore, as actual members of the Catholic Church, and will not be deprived of communion with the Church, nor of the rights, which through this communion, accrue to us in Church and State.

We declare the ecclesiastical penalties decreed against us, on account of our fidelity to our creed, to be unjustifiable and tyrannical; and we will not allow ourselves to be daunted or hindered by these censures in availing ourselves of our communion with the Church according to our conscience. From the point of view of the confession of faith contained in the so-called Tridentine Creed, we repudiate the dogmas introduced under the pontificate of Pius IX in contradiction to the doctrine of the Church, and to the principles continuously followed since the Council of Jerusalem, especially the dogmas of the Pope's infallible teaching, and of his supreme episcopal and immediate jurisdiction.

2. We rely on the old constitution of the Church. We protest against every attempt to oust the bishops from the immediate and independent control of the separate Churches. We repudiate, as in conflict with the Tridentine Canon, according to which there exists a God-appointed hierarchy of bishops, priests, and deacons, the doctrine embodied in the Vatican

doctrine, that the Pope is the sole God-appointed depositary of all ecclesiastical authority and power. We recognize the primacy of the Bishop of Rome as it was acknowledged, on authority of Scripture, by Fathers and Councils in the old undivided Christian Church.

a. We declare that articles of belief cannot be defined merely by the utterance of the Pope for the time being, and the express or tacit assent of the bishops, bound as they are by oath to unqualified obedience to the Pope; but only in accordance with Holy Scripture and the old tradition of the Church, as it is set forth in the recognized Fathers and Councils. Moreover a council which was not, as the Vatican Council was, deficient in the actual external conditions of oecuminicity, but which, in the general sentiment of its members, exhibited a disregard of the fundamental principles and of the past history of the Church, could not issue decrees binding upon the consciences of the members of the Church.

b. We lay stress upon this principle that the conformity of the doctrinal decisions of a council, with the primitive and traditional creed of the Church, must be determined by the consciousness of belief of the Catholic people and by theological science. We maintain for the Catholic laity and the clergy, as well as for theological sciences, the right of testifying and of objecting on the occasion of establishing articles of belief.

3. We aim at a reform in the Church in cooperation with the sciences of theology and canon law,

which shall, in the spirit of the ancient Church, remove the present defects and abuses, and in particular shall fulfill the legitimate decrees of the Catholic people for a constitutionally regulated participation in Church business, whereby, without risk to doctrinal unity or doctrine, national considerations and needs may be taken account of.

We declare that the charge of Jansenism against the Church of Utrecht is unfounded, and that consequently no opposition in dogma exists between it and us.

We hope for a reunion with the Greco-oriental and Russian Church, the separation of which had no sufficient origin, and depends upon no insuperable difference in dogma. Whilst pursuing the desired reforms in the path of science and a progressive Christian culture, we hope gradually to bring about a good understanding with the Protestant and Episcopal churches.

4. We hold scientific study indispensable for the training of the clergy.

We consider that the artificial seclusion of the clergy from the intellectual culture of the present century (as in the seminaries and higher schools under the sole conduct of the bishops) is dangerous, from the great influence which the clergy possess over the culture of the people, and that it is altogether unsuited to give the clergy such an education and training as shall combine piety and morality, intellectual culture and patriotic feeling. We claim for the lower order of clergy a suitable position of consideration, protected against all hierarchical tyranny.

We protest against the arbitrary removal of secular priests, *amovibilitas ad nutum*, a practice introduced through the French Code, and latterly imposed everywhere.

5. We support the constitutions of our countries, which secure us civil freedom and culture. Therefore we repudiate on national and historical grounds the dangerous dogma of Papal supremacy; and promise to stand faithfully and resolutely by our respective Governments in the struggle against that Ultramontanism which assumes the form of dogma in the Syllabus.

6. Since manifestly the present miserable confusion in the Church has been occasioned by the society called that of Jesus; since this order abuses its influence to spread and cherish among the hierarchy, clergy, and people, tendencies hostile to culture, dangerous to the State and to the nation; since it teaches and encourages a false and corrupting morality: we declare it as our conviction that peace and prosperity, unity in the Church, and just relations between her and civil society, will only be possible when the pernicious activity of this order is put an end to.

7. As members of the Catholic Church, to which—not yet altered by the Vatican decrees—Government had guaranteed political recognition and public protection, we maintain our claims to all the real property and legal rights of the Church.

the fourteen theses of the old catholic union conference at bonn—september 14-16, 1874

I. WE AGREE THAT THE APOCRYPHAL or deutero-canonical books of the Old Testament are not of the same canonicity as the books contained in the Hebrew Canon.

II. We agree that no translation of Holy Scripture can claim an authority superior to that of the original text.

III. We agree that the reading of Holy Scripture in the vulgar tongue cannot be lawfully forbidden.

IV. We agree that, in general, it is more fitting, and in accordance with the spirit of the Church, that the Liturgy should be in the tongue understood by the people.

V. We agree that Faith working by Love, not Faith without Love, is the means and condition of Man's justification before God.

VI. Salvation cannot be merited by "merit of condignity," because there is no proportion between the infinite worth of salvation promised by God and the finite worth of man's works.

VII. We agree that the doctrine of *"opera supererogationis"* and of a *"thesaurus meritorium sanctorum,"* i.e., that the overflowing merits of the Saints can be transferred to others, either by the rulers of the Church, or by the authors of the good works themselves, is untenable.

VIII. 1. We acknowledge that the number of sacraments was fixed at seven, first in the twelfth century, and then was received into the general teaching of the Church, not as a tradition coming down from the Apostles or from the earliest of times, but as the result of theological speculation.

2. Catholic theologians acknowledge, and we acknowledge with them, that Baptism and the Eucharist are *"principalia, praecipus, eximia salutis nostrae sacramenta."*

IX. 1. The Holy Scriptures being recognized as the primary rule of Faith, we agree that the genuine tradition, *i.e.* the unbroken transmission partly oral, partly in writing of the doctrine delivered by Christ and the Apostles is an authoritative source of teaching for all successive generations of Christians. This tradition is partly to be found in the consensus of the great ecclesiastical bodies standing in historical continuity with the primitive Church, partly to be gathered by scientific method from the written documents of all centuries.

2. We acknowledge that the Church of England; and the Churches derived through her, have maintained unbroken the Episcopal succession.

X. We reject the new Roman doctrine of the Immaculate Conception of the Blessed Virgin Mary, as being contrary to the tradition of the first thirteen centuries, according to which Christ alone is conceived without sin.

XI. We agree that the practice of confession of sins before the congregation or a Priest, together with the exercise of the power of the keys, has come down to us from the primitive Church, and that, purged from abuses and free from constraint, it should be preserved in the Church.

XII. We agree that "indulgences" can only refer to penalties actually imposed by the Church herself.

XIII. We acknowledge that the practice of the commemoration of the faithful departed, i.e. the calling down of a richer outpouring of Christ's grace upon them, has come down to us from the primitive Church, and is to be preserved in the Church.

XIV. 1. The Eucharistic celebration in the Church is not a continuous repetition or renewal of the propitiatory sacrifice offered once forever by Christ upon the cross; but its sacrificial character consists in this, that it is the permanent memorial of it, and a representation and presentation on earth of that one oblation of Christ for the salvation of redeemed mankind, which according to the Epistle to the Hebrews (9:11, 12), is continuously presented in heaven by Christ, who now appears in the presence of God for us (9:24).

2. While this is the character of the Eucharist in reference to the sacrifice of Christ, it is also a sacred feast, wherein the faithful, receiving the Body and Blood of our Lord, have communion one with another (I Cor. 10:17).

declaration of utrecht
written by utrecht union bishops—1889

1. WE ADHERE FAITHFULLY to the Rule of Faith laid down by St. Vincent of Lerins in these terms: *"Id teneamus, quod ubique, quod semper, quod ab omnibus creditum est; hoc est eternim vere proprieque catholicum."* For this reason we persevere in professing the faith of the primitive Church, as formulated in the œcumenical symbols and specified precisely by the unanimously accepted decisions of the Œcumenical Councils held in the undivided Church of the first thousand years.

2. We therefore reject the decrees of the so-called Council of the Vatican, which were promulgated July 18th, 1870, concerning the infallibility and the Universal Episcopate of the Bishop of Rome, decrees which are in contradiction with the faith of the ancient Church, and which destroy its ancient canonical constitution by attributing to the Pope the plenitude of ecclesiastical powers over all Dioceses and over all the faithful. By denial of this primatial jurisdiction we do not wish to deny the historical primacy which several Œcumenical Councils and Fathers of the ancient Church have attributed to the Bishop of Rome by recognizing him as the *Primus inter pares.*

3. We also reject the dogma of the Immaculate Conception promulgated by Pius IX in 1854 in defiance of the Holy Scriptures and in contradiction to the tradition of the centuries.

4. As for other Encyclicals published by the Bishops of Rome in recent times, for example, the Bulls

Unigenitus and *Auctorem fidei,* and the Syllabus of 1864, we reject them on all such points as are in contradiction with the doctrine of the primitive Church and we do not recognize them as binding on the consciences of the faithful. We also renew the ancient protests of the Catholic Church of Holland against the errors of the Roman Curia, and against its attacks upon the rights of national Churches.

5. We refuse to accept the decrees of the Council of Trent in matters of discipline, and as for the dogmatic decisions of that Council we accept them only so far as they are in harmony with the teaching of the primitive Church.

6. Considering that the Holy Eucharist has always been the true central point of Catholic worship, we consider it our right to declare that we maintain with perfect fidelity the ancient Catholic doctrine concerning the Sacrament of the Altar, by believing that we receive the Body and Blood of our Saviour Jesus Christ under the species of bread and wine. The Eucharistic celebration in the Church is neither a continual repetition nor a renewal of the expiatory sacrifice which Jesus offered once for all upon the Cross: but it is a sacrifice because it is the perpetual commemoration of the sacrifice offered upon the Cross, and it is the act by which we represent upon earth and appropriate to ourselves the one offering which Jesus Christ makes in Heaven, according to the Epistle to the Hebrews 9:11-12, for the salvation of redeemed humanity, by appearing for us in the presence of God (Heb. 9:24). The character of the Holy Eucharist being thus under-

stood, it is, at the same time, a sacrificial feast, by means of which the faithful in receiving the Body and Blood of our Saviour, enter into communion with one another (I Cor.10:17).

7. We hope that Catholic theologians, in maintaining the faith of the undivided Church, will succeed in establishing an agreement upon questions which have been controverted ever since the divisions which arose between the Churches. We exhort the priests under our jurisdiction to teach, both by preaching and by the instruction of the young, especially the essential Christian truths professed by all the Christian confessions, to avoid, in discussing controverted doctrines, any violation of truth or charity, and in word and deed to set an example to the members.

8. By maintaining and professing faithfully the doctrine of Jesus Christ, by refusing to admit those errors which by the fault of men have crept into the Catholic Church, by laying aside the abuses in ecclesiastical matters, together with the worldly tendencies of the hierarchy, we believe that we shall be able to combat efficaciously the great evils of our day, which are unbelief and indifference in matters of religion.

Utrecht, 24th September 1889

+Heykam
+Rinkel
+Diependaal
+Reinkens
+Herzog

the declaration of autonomy
by the most reverend arnold arris mathew, 1910

Reprinted from "An Episcopal Odyssey" by Arnold Harris Mathew, Archbishop of the Old Roman Catholic Rite in Great Britain and Ireland, November 1, 1915.

WE THE UNDERSIGNED BISHOP, on behalf of our clergy and laity of the Catholic Church of England, hereby proclaim and declare the autonomy and independence of our portion of the One, Holy, Catholic and Apostolic Church. We are in no way whatever subject to or dependent upon any foreign See, nor do we recognize the right of any members of the religious bodies known as "Old Catholics" on the Continent, to require submission from us to their authority or jurisdiction, or the decrees, decisions, rules or assemblies, in which we have neither taken part nor expressed agreement.

We had supposed and believed that the Faith, once delivered to the Saints, and set forth in the decrees of the Councils accepted as Ecumenical no less in the West than in the East, would have continued unimpaired, whether by augmentation or by diminution, in the venerable Church of the Dutch Nation.

We anticipated that the admirable fidelity with which the Bishops and Clergy of that Church had adhered to the Faith and handed it down, untarnished by heresy, notwithstanding grievous persecution during so many centuries, would never have wavered.

Unfortunately, however, we discover with dismay,

pain, and regret that the standards of orthodoxy, laid down of old by the Fathers and Councils of the East and West alike, having been departed from in various particulars by certain sections of Old Catholicism, these departures, instead of being checked and repressed, are, at least tacitly, tolerated and acquiesced in without protest, by the Hierarchy of the Church of the Netherlands.

In order to avoid misapprehension, we here specify nine of the points of difference between Continental Old Catholics and ourselves:

(1) Although the Synod of Jerusalem, held under Dositheus in 1672, was not an Ecumenical Council, its decrees are accepted by the Holy Orthodox Church of the Orient as accurately expressing its belief, and are in harmony with the decrees of the Council of Trent on the dogmas of which they treat. We are in agreement with the Holy Orthodox Church, regarding this Synod, hence, we hold and declare that there are Seven Holy Mysteries or Sacraments instituted by Our Divine Lord and Savior Jesus Christ, therefore all of them necessary for the salvation of mankind, though all are not necessarily to be received by every individual, e.g. Holy Orders and Matrimony. Certain sections, if not all, of the Old Catholic bodies, reject this belief and refuse to assent to the decrees of the Holy Synod of Jerusalem.

(2) Moreover, some of them have abolished the Sacrament of Penance by condemning and doing away with auricular confession; others actively discourage this salutary practice; others, again, whilst tolerating

its use, declare the Sacrament of Penance to be merely optional, therefore unnecessary, and of no obligation, even for those who have fallen into mortal sin after Baptism.

(3) In accordance with the belief and practice of the Universal Church, we adhere to the doctrine of the Communion of Saints by invoking and venerating the Blessed Virgin Mary, and those who have received the crown of glory in heaven, as well as the Holy Angels of God. The Old Catholics in the Netherlands have not yet altogether abandoned this pious and helpful custom, but, in some other countries, invocation of the Saints has been totally abolished by the Old Catholics.

(4) Although it may be permissible and indeed, very desirable, in some countries, and, under certain circumstances, to render the Liturgy into the vernacular languages, we consider it to be neither expedient nor tolerable that individuals should compose new liturgies, according to their own particular views, or make alterations, omissions, and changes in venerable rites to suit their peculiar fancies, prejudices, or idiosyncrasies. We lament the mutilations of this kind which have occurred among the Old Catholics in several countries and regret that no two of the new liturgies composed and published by them are alike, either in form or in ceremony. In all of them the ancient rubrics have been set aside, and the ceremonies and symbolism with which the Sacred Mysteries of the Altar have been reverently environed for many centuries, have, either wholly or in part, been ruthlessly swept away. The Rite of Benediction of the Blessed Sacrament has

also been almost universally abolished among the Old Catholics.

(5) In accordance with the primitive teaching of the Church of the Netherlands, which prevailed until a very recent date, we consider it a duty on the part of Western Christians to remember His Holiness the Pope as their Patriarch in their prayers and sacrifices. The name of His Holiness should, therefore, retain its position in the Canon of the Mass, where, as we observed at our consecration in Utrecht, it was customary, and remained so until a recent date in the present year (1910), for the celebrant to recite the name of our Patriarch in the usual manner in the Mass and in the Litany of the Saints. The publication of a new vernacular Dutch Liturgy in the present year causes us to regret that the clergy of Holland are now required to omit the name of His Holiness in the Canon of the Mass. Happily, only a small number of other alterations in the text of the Canon have, so far, been introduced. These include the omission of the title, 'ever Virgin' whenever it occurs in the Latin Missal. Such alterations pave the way for others of an even more serious nature, which may be made in the future, and, as we think, are to be deplored.

(6) Following the example of our Catholic forefathers, we venerate the adorable Sacrifice of the Mass as the supreme act of Christian worship instituted by Christ Himself. We grieve that the Old Catholic clergy, in most countries, have abandoned the daily celebration of Mass, and now limit the offering of the Christian Sacrifice to Sundays and a few of the greater

Feasts. The corresponding neglect of the Blessed Sacrament, and infrequency of Holy Communion, on the part of the laity, are marked.

(7) In accordance with Catholic custom and with the decrees of the Ecumenical Councils, we hold that the honor and glory of God are promoted and increased by the devout and religious use of holy pictures, statues, symbols, relics, and the like, as aids to devotion, and that, in relations to those they represent, they are to be held in veneration. The Old Catholics have, generally speaking, preferred to dispense with such helps to piety.

(8) We consider that the Holy Sacraments should be administered only to those who are members of the Holy Catholic Church, not only by Baptism, but by the profession of the Catholic Faith in its integrity. Unhappily, we find persons who are not Catholics are now admitted to receive Holy Communion in all Old Catholic places of worship on the Continent.

(9) The Old Catholics have ceased to observe the prescribed days of fasting and abstinence, and no longer observe the custom of receiving Holy Communion fasting.

For these and other reasons, which it is unnecessary to detail, we, the undersigned Bishop, desire, by these presents, to declare our autonomy and our independence of all foreign interference in our doctrine, discipline, and policy. *In necessaries unites, in dubiis libertes, in omnibus caritas.*

+*Arnold Harris Mathew*

catholic jurisdictions

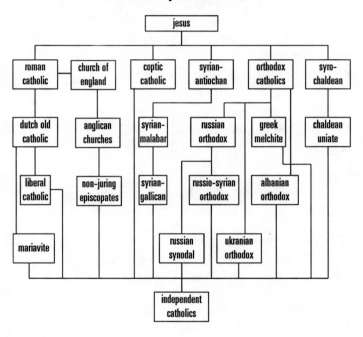

*Adapted from the Apostolic Lineage chart developed by the
White Robed Monks of St. Benedict (www.whiterobedmonks.org).*

apostolic succession

Every jurisdiction keeps careful track of its own apostolic succession. The succession below is included only as an example. It begins with a bishop of the Roman Catholic Church, which holds an undisputed claim to apostolic succession, and ends with the late Herman Adrian Spruit, Patriarch of the Church of Antioch. Spruit sought to consolidate the various streams of apostolic succession into one line, of which this is only one example. Most independent jurisdictions share Spruit's legacy or at least some point of contact with this lineage.

On 12 March 1566,
Cardinal Scipione Rebiba,
Roman Catholic Bishop of Troia, consecrated

Giulio Antonio Santorio,
Roman Catholic Archbishop of Santa Severina,
who on 7 September 1586 consecrated

Girolamo Bernerio, O.P.,
Roman Catholic Bishop of Ascoli Piceno,
who on 4 April 1604 consecrated

Galeazzo Sanvitale,
Roman Catholic Archbishop of Bari,
who on 2 May 1621 consecrated

Ludovico Ludovisi,
Roman Catholic Archbishop of Bologna,
who on 12 June 1622 consecrated

Luigi Caetani,
Roman Catholic Titular Patriarch of Antioch,
who on 7 October 1630 consecrated

Giovanni Battista Scannaroli,
Roman Catholic Titular Bishop of Sidon,
who on 24 October 1655 consecrated

Antonio Barberini (the younger),
Roman Catholic Bishop of Frascati,
who on 11 November 1668 consecrated

Charles Maurice Le Tellier
Roman Catholic Bishop of Mieux,
who on 21 September 1670 consecrated

Jaques Benigne Boussuet
who on 24 October 1693 consecrated

Jaques Goyon De Matigon,
who on 18 February 1719 consecrated

Dominicus Marie Varlet,
Roman Catholic Bishop of Babylon,
who on 17 October 1739 consecrated

Petrus Meindaerts
Old Catholic Archbishop of Utrecht,
who on 11 July 1745 consecrated

Johannes Van Stiphout,
Old Catholic Bishop of Haarlem,
who on 7 February 1768 consecrated

Gualterus Michael Van Nieuwenhuizen,
Old Catholic Archbishop of Utrecht,
who on 21 June 1778 consecrated

Adrianus Johannes Broekman,
Old Catholic Bishop of Haarlem,
who on 5 July 1797 consecrated

Johannes Jacobus Van Rhijn,
Old Catholic Archbishop of Utrecht,
who on 7 November 1805 consecrated

Gilbert Cornelius De Jong,
Old Catholic Bishop of Deventer,
who on 24 April 1814 consecrated

Willibord Van Os,
Old Catholic Archbishop of Utrecht,
who on 25 April 1819 consecrated

Johannes Bon,
Old Catholic Bishop of Haarlem,
who on 13 November 1824 consecrated

Johannes Van Santen,
Old Catholic Archbishop of Utrecht,
who on 17 July 1854 consecrated

Casparus Johannes Rinkel,
Old Catholic Bishop of Haarlem,
who on 11 May 1892 consecrated

Gerard Gul,
Old Catholic Archbishop of Utrecht,
who on 28 April 1908 consecrated

Arnold Harris Mathew,
Old Catholic Bishop for Great Britain,
who on 28 October 1914 consecrated

Frederick Samuel Willoughby,
who on 13 February 1916 consecrated

James Ingall Wedgwood,
Presiding Bishop of the Liberal Catholic Church,
who on 13 July 1919 consecrated

Irving Steiger Cooper,
Liberal Catholic Regionary Bishop for the United
States, who on 13 September 1931 consecrated

Charles H. Hampton,
Liberal Catholic Regionary Bishop for the United
States, who on 22 June 1957 consecrated

Herman Adrian Spruit,
who became Archbishop-Patriarch of the Church
of Antioch (Catholic Apostolic Church of Antioch,
Malabar Rite)

notes

1   For instance, it was not until the Council of Nicea
     in the year 325 that the church came to a final
     decision on Jesus' divinity. There have also been
     a variety of theories of the atonement through the
     church's history (such as the Ransom theory, the
     Christus Victor theory, and the Commercial the-
     ory, to name just a few), as well as differing inter-
     pretations of the Eucharist and other sacraments,
     all of which have been understood as orthodox or
     "correct teaching."

2   I (John M.) am indebted to the Most Rev. Robert
     Dittler, PhD for this insight.

about the authors

JOHN PLUMMER holds a Master's degree in Historical Theology from Vanderbilt University and a doctorate in Theological Studies from the Graduate Theological Foundation. He is the author of *The Many Paths of the Independent Sacramental Movement* and *Living Mysteries: a Practical Handbook for the Independent Priest.* He is an Independent Catholic bishop, and his ministry is independent of any specific jurisdiction. In addition to his primary ministry, he is also the assistant bishop for North America for the Apostolic Church of the Risen Christ. He lives with his family in Nashville, Tennessee.

JOHN R. MABRY holds a Master's degree in Creation Spirituality from Holy Names College and a doctorate in Philosophy and Religion from the California Institute of Integral Studies. He has served as editor for *Creation Spirituality* magazine, and *Presence: An International Journal of Spiritual Direction,* and as managing editor for the Episcopal Diocese of California's *Pacific Church News.* He currently serves as co-pastor of Grace North Church in Berkeley, CA, a consensus liturgical community, and as Director of the Interfaith Spiritual Direction Certificate Program at the Chaplaincy Institute for Arts and Interfaith Ministry, where he also teaches world religions and interfaith theology. He is the author of *Faith Styles: Ways People Believe; Noticing the Divine: An Introduction to Interfaith Spiritual Guidance; God As Nature Sees God: A Christian Reading of the Tao Te Ching; Heretics, Mystics & Misfits;* and *Crisis and Communion: The Remythologization of the Eucharist.* He lives in the San Francisco Bay Area. Visit his website at www.apocryphile.org/jrm/.

Printed in the United States
90560LV00001B/64/A

9 781933 993003